TO: _____

FROM: _____

Come to me, all you who are weary and burdened,

and I will give you rest.

—Matthew 11:28

Adaptation *Finding God's Peace and Joy*
Copyright © 1999 by The Zondervan Corporation
ISBN 0-310-97959-5

Excerpts taken from:
Streams in the Desert, Updated Edition
Edited by James Reimann
Copyright © 1997 by The Zondervan Corporation.
Adapted from *Finding Peace* and *Discovering Joy*

Published under license from ZondervanPublishingHouse.

Photos: ©William J. Hebert
        ©Dennis Frates/Oregon Scenics

Printed in China
99 00 01 /HK/ 5 4 3 2

FINDING GOD'S

peace & joy

Adapted from *Finding Peace* and *Discovering Joy*

Edited by James Reimann
Photography by William J. Hebert and Dennis Frates

BOOKS ⚊ Zondervan

BOK3012

FINDING

peace

The Lord is to be our source of supply.

In him are springs, fountains, and streams

that will never be cut off or run dry.

To those who are anxious comes the

gracious promise of our heavenly Father:

If he is the source of our mercies, mercy

will never fail us.

IN THE WILDERNESS SHALL WATERS BREAK OUT,

AND STREAMS IN THE DESERT.

—Isaiah 35:6 KJV

"My peace I give you." —John 14:27

Two painters were once asked to paint a picture illustrating their own ideas of rest. *The first chose for his scene a quiet, lonely lake, nestled among mountains far away.* The second, using swift, broad strokes on his canvas, painted a thundering waterfall. Beneath the falls grew a fragile birch tree, bending over the foam. *On its branches, nearly wet with the spray from the falls, sat a robin on its nest.* The first painting was simply a picture of stagnation and inactivity. *The second, however, depicted rest.*

—Drummond

THE PEACE OF GOD, WHICH TRANSCENDS

ALL UNDERSTANDING, WILL GUARD YOUR HEARTS

AND YOUR MINDS IN CHRIST JESUS.

—Philippians 4:7

When God is the center of a soul, although disasters may crowd in on all sides and roar like the waves of the sea, there is a constant calm within. The world can neither give nor take away this kind of peace.

— Archbishop Leighton

God gives quietness in the midst of the raging storm.... *He waves his hand, signaling the end of the raging tempest and the beginning of the restful calm.* His voice is heard above the screaming of the wind through the ropes and rigging, and over the thrashing of the waves. *"Quiet! Be still!"* (Mark 4:39). Can you not hear it? *And instantly there is a great calm.*

God giveth quietness. —Job 34:29 KJV

SURELY I AM WITH YOU ALWAYS.

—Matthew 28:20

Do not look ahead to what may happen tomorrow. The same everlasting Father who cares for you today will take care of you tomorrow and every day. Either he will shield you from suffering or he will give you his unwavering strength that you may bear it. Be at peace, then, and set aside all anxious thoughts and worries.

—Frances de Sales

Let him who walks in the dark, who has no light,
trust in the name of the Lord. —Isaiah 50:10

Only the peace of God will quiet our minds and put our hearts at rest. *We must place our hand in his as a little child and allow him to lead us into the bright sunshine of his love.* He knows the way out of the dense, dark forest, so may we climb into his arms, trusting him to rescue us by showing us the shortest and most reliable road.

—Dr. Pardington

One of the blessings of the old-time Sabbath day was the calmness, restfulness, and holy peace that came from having a time of quiet solitude away from the world. There is a special strength that is born in solitude. Crows travel in flocks, and wolves in packs, but the lion and the eagle are usually found alone.

JESUS WENT UP ON A

MOUNTAINSIDE BY HIMSELF.

—Matthew 14:23

"Be still, and know that I am God." —Psalm 46:10

Place the storm of your individual troubles on God's altar of everyday trials, and the same night, the Lord will appear to you. *His rainbow will extend across the subsiding flood, and in your stillness you will hear the everlasting music.*

—George Matheson

MAY GOD HIMSELF, THE GOD OF PEACE,

SANCTIFY YOU THROUGH AND THROUGH.

—1 Thessalonians 5:23

Holiness makes the soul like a field or garden of God,

with every kind of pleasant fruit and flower, and each

one delightful and undisturbed, enjoying a sweet calm

and the gentle and refreshing rays of the sun.

—Jonathan Edwards

Dew will never appear while there is either heat or wind. *The temperature must fall, the wind cease, and the air come to a point of coolness and rest—absolute rest—before the invisible particles of moisture will become dew to dampen any plant or flower.* And the grace of God does not come forth to bring rest and renewal to our soul until we completely reach the point of stillness before him.

"This is the resting place,

let the weary rest." —Isaiah 28:12

GOD'S COMMAND, "DO NOT BE ANXIOUS
ABOUT ANYTHING" (PHILIPPIANS 4:6),
IS UNLIMITED, AND SO IS THE VERSE,
"CAST ALL YOUR ANXIETY ON HIM" (1 PETER 5:7).
—Dr. Payson

What I really needed was the deep ocean of
God's love, and the high mountains of his truth
within me. His wisdom had depths and heights
that neither the ocean nor the mountains could
contain and that could not be compared with
jewels, gold, or precious stones.

—Margaret Bottome

L~ORD~, you have been our dwelling place throughout all generations. —Psalm 90:1

God is your Father. *Can you state that truth with full assurance and faith?* Once you do, your dove of faith will no longer wander the skies in restless flight but will settle forever in its eternal resting place of peace: your Father!

—Arthur Christopher Bacon

Dear Father, I am coming to meet with you.

Nothing on the common, everyday plain of life

will keep me away from your holy heights. At

your calling I come, so I have the assurance

that you will meet with me. Each morning

begun so well on the mountain will make me

strong and glad the rest of the day!

—Joseph Parker

peace

GOD IS OUR REFUGE AND STRENGTH,

AN EVER-PRESENT HELP IN TROUBLE.

—Psalm 46:1

Isaac went out to the field

one evening to meditate. —Genesis 24:63

People living in cities today would do well to follow the example of Isaac and as often as possible visit the fields of the countryside, away from the hustle and bustle of the city.... *A walk through a field, a stroll by a seashore, or a hike across a meadow sprinkled with daisies will purge you of the impurities of life and will cause your heart to beat with new joy and hope.*

WHERE MORNING DAWNS AND EVENING FADES

YOU CALL FORTH SONGS OF JOY.

—Psalm 65:8

Have you ever risen early, climbed a hill, and watched God make a morning? The dull gray gives way as he pushes the sun toward the horizon, and then the tints and hues of every color begin to blend into one perfect light as the full sun suddenly bursts into view. As king of the day, the sun moves majestically across the sky, flooding the earth and every deep valley with glorious light. At this point, you can hear the music of heaven's choir as it sings of the majesty of God himself and of the glory of the morning.

Being restless and having worries and cares are absolutely forbidden by our Lord, who said, "So do not worry, saying, 'What shall we eat?' or 'What shall we drink?' or 'What shall we wear?'" (Matthew 6:31). *He does not mean that we are not to think ahead or that our life should never have a plan or pattern to it. He simply means that we are not to worry about these things.*

—the Rev. Darlow Sargeant

May your unfailing love rest upon us, O LORD, even as we put our hope in you. —Psalm 33:22

MY PEACE I GIVE WHEN PRAYER

SEEMS LOST, UNHEARD;

KNOW MY PROMISES ARE EVER IN MY WORD.

All the peace, happiness, and power of the Christian life hinges on one thing. That one thing is taking God at his Word, believing he really means exactly what he says.

—Frances Ridley Havergal

The LORD longs to be gracious to you;

he rises to show you compassion. —Isaiah 30:18

The greenest grass is found wherever the most rain falls. So I suppose it is the fog and mist of Ireland that makes it "the Emerald Isle." *And wherever you find the widespread fog of trouble and the mist of sorrow, you always find emerald green hearts that are full of the beautiful foliage of the comfort and love of God.*

—Charles H. Spurgeon

There is nothing that makes the Scriptures more precious to us than a time of "captivity." The old psalms of God's Word have sung for us with compassion by our stream at Babel and have resounded with new joy as we have seen the Lord deliver us from captivity and "restore our fortunes, … like streams in the Negev" (Psalm 126:4).

—William Taylor

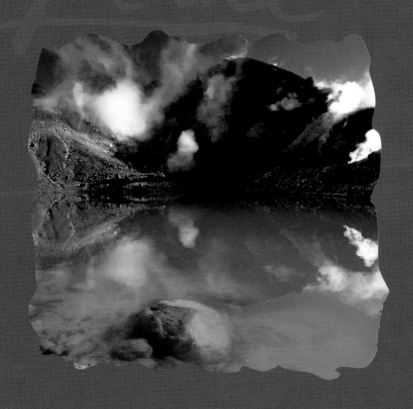

"ALL MY SPRINGS OF JOY ARE IN YOU."

—Psalm 87:7 NASB

his my song through endless ages,

Jesus led me all the way.

The shepherds of the Alps have a beautiful custom of ending the day by singing an evening farewell to one another. *The air is so pure that the songs can be heard for very long distances.* As the sun begins to set, they gather their flocks and begin to lead them down the mountain paths while they sing, *"'Thus far has the LORD helped us.'"(1 Samuel 7:12)* Let us praise his name!

"COME, COME," HE CALLS YOU,

"O SOUL OPPRESSED AND WEARY,

COME TO THE SHADOWS OF MY DESERT REST;

COME WALK WITH ME FAR

FROM LIFE'S NOISY DISCORDS,

AND PEACE WILL BREATHE

LIKE MUSIC IN YOUR BREAST."

Be all at rest, so then you'll be an answer

To those who question,

"Who is God and where?"

For God is rest, and where he dwells is stillness,

And they who dwell in him,

his rest will share.

And what will meet the deep unrest around you,

But the calm peace of God

that filled his breast?

For still a living voice calls to the weary,

From him who said,

"Come unto me and rest."

—Freda Hanbury Allen

Though the fig tree does not bud and there are no grapes on the vines, *though the olive crop fails and the fields produce no food,* though there are no sheep in the pen and no cattle in the stalls, *yet I will rejoice in the LORD, I will be joyful in God my Savior.*

—Habbakuk 3:17–18

Don't you know that day dawns after night, showers displace drought, and spring and summer follow winter? Then, have hope! Hope forever, for God will not fail you!

—Charles H. Spurgeon

THE LORD GIVES STRENGTH TO HIS PEOPLE;
THE LORD BLESSES HIS PEOPLE WITH PEACE.

—Psalm 29:11

DISCOVERING

joy

joy

You have made known to me the path of life;

you will fill me with joy in your presence,

with eternal pleasures at your right hand.

—Psalm 16:11

Lift up your eyes...

All the land that you see I will give to you.

—Genesis 13:14-15

Everything you can comprehend through faith's vision belongs to you. Look as far as you can, for it is all yours. All you long to be as a Christian, and all you long to do for God, are within the possibilities of faith. Then draw closer to him, and with your Bible before you, and your soul completely open to the power of the Spirit, allow your entire being to receive the baptism of his presence.

Do you not know?

Have you not heard?

The LORD is the everlasting God,

the Creator of the ends of the earth.

He will not grow tired or weary,

and his understanding no one can fathom.

He gives strength to the weary

and increases the power of the weak.

Even youths grow tired and weary,

and young men stumble and fall;

but those who hope in the LORD

will renew their strength.

They will soar on wings like eagles;

they will run and not grow weary,

they will walk and not be faint.

—Isaiah 40:28-31

joy

STAND FIRM AND YOU WILL SEE THE
DELIVERANCE THE LORD WILL BRING YOU TODAY.
—Exodus 14:13

By faith we eagerly await through the Spirit

the righteousness for which we hope.

—Galatians 5:5

If I see God in everything, he will calm and color everything I see! Perhaps the circumstances causing my sorrows will not be removed and my situation will remain the same, but if Christ is brought into my grief and gloom as my Lord and Master, he will "surround me with songs of deliverance" (Psalm 32:7).

—Hannah Whitall Smith

God is in every tomorrow,

Therefore I live for today,

Certain of finding at sunrise,

Guidance and strength for my way;

Power for each moment of weakness,

Hope for each moment of pain,

Comfort for every sorrow,

Sunshine and joy after rain.

THANKS BE TO GOD, WHO ALWAYS LEADS US
IN TRIUMPHAL PROCESSION IN CHRIST.

—2 Corinthians 2:14

Rejoice in the Lord always.

I will say it again: Rejoice! —Philippians 4:4

I still believe that a day of understanding will come for each of us, however far away it may be. *We will understand as we see the tragedies that today darken and dampen the presence of heaven for us take their proper place in God's great plan—a plan so overwhelming, magnificent, and joyful, we will laugh with wonder and delight.*

—Arthur Christopher Bacon

Oh, let us rejoice in the Lord, evermore,

When darts of the Tempter are flying,

For Satan still dreads, as he oft did before,

Our singing much more than our sighing.

Be filled with the Spirit.... Sing and make music in

your heart to the Lord.

—Ephesians 5:18–19

The LORD is my strength and my shield;

my heart trusts in him, and I am helped.

My heart leaps for joy and

I will give thanks to him in song.

—Psalm 28:7

It is said that springs of sweet, fresh water pool up amid the saltiness of the oceans, that the fairest Alpine flowers bloom in the wildest and most rugged mountain passes, and that the most magnificent psalms arose from the most profound agonies of the soul. *May it continue to be!* Therefore, amid a multitude of trials, souls who love God will discover reasons for boundless, leaping joy.

—from *Tried as by Fire*

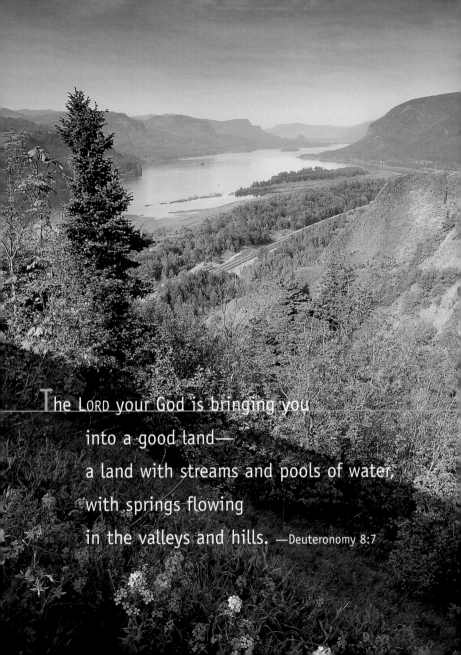

The LORD your God is bringing you
into a good land—
a land with streams and pools of water,
with springs flowing
in the valleys and hills. —Deuteronomy 8:7

THE EAGLE THAT SOARS

AT GREAT ALTITUDES

DOES NOT WORRY ABOUT

HOW IT WILL CROSS A RIVER.

It is easier to sing your worries away than to reason them away. Why not sing in the morning? Think of the birds—they are the first to sing each day, and they have fewer worries than anything else in creation. And don't forget to sing in the evening, which is what the robins do when they have finished their daily work. Once they have flown their last flight of the day and gathered the last bit of food, they find a treetop from which to sing a song of praise.

This is exactly how God deals with every child of his when we truly sacrifice. *We surrender everything we own and accept poverty—then he sends wealth....* We surrender all our cherished hopes and die to self—then he sends overflowing joy.

—Dr. C. G. Trumbull

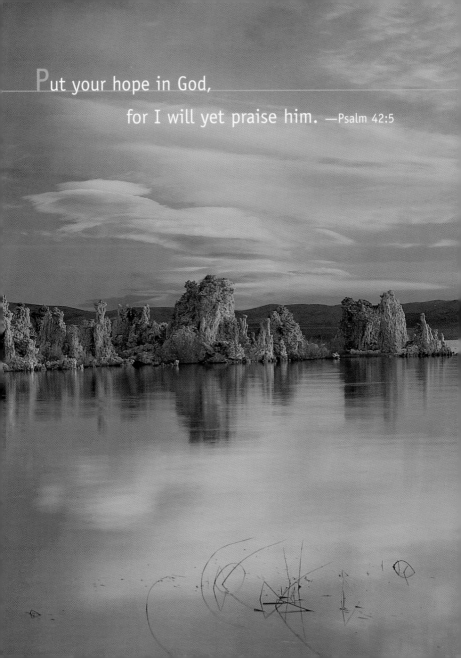

Put your hope in God,

for I will yet praise him. —Psalm 42:5

The Lord is sure to accomplish those things,

O trusting heart, the Lord to you has told;

Let faith and hope arise, and lift their wings,

To soar toward the sunrise clouds of gold;

The doorways of the rosy dawn swing wide,

Revealing joys the darkness of night did hide.

—Bessie Porter

WHEN THE LORD CALLS YOU

TO COME ACROSS THE WATER,

STEP OUT WITH CONFIDENCE AND JOY.

AND NEVER GLANCE AWAY FROM HIM

FOR EVEN A MOMENT.

I have learned to love the darkness of sorrow,

for it is there I see

the brightness of God's face.

—Madame Guyon

Nothing that is not part of God's will is allowed to come into the life of someone who trusts and obeys him. *This truth should be enough to make our life one of ceaseless thanksgiving and joy, because God's will is the most hopeful, pleasant, and glorious thing in the world.*

—H. W. S.

If I experience the presence of God in his majesty through my pain and loss, so that I bow before him and pray,

"Your will be done" (Matthew 6:10),

then I have gained much indeed. God gave Job glimpses of his future glory, for in those weary and difficult days and nights, he was allowed to penetrate God's veil and could honestly say,

"I know that my Redeemer lives" (Job 19:25).

—from *In the Hour of Silence*

THEN JOB REPLIED TO THE LORD:

"I KNOW THAT YOU CAN DO ALL THINGS;

NO PLAN OF YOURS CAN BE THWARTED."

—Job 42:1-2

"Until now you have not
asked for anything in my name.
Ask and you will receive,
and your joy will be complete."

—John 16:24

I like to cultivate the spirit of happiness! *It retunes my soul and keeps it so perfectly in tune that Satan is afraid to touch it.* The chords of my soul become so vibrant and full of heavenly electricity that he takes his fiendish fingers from me and goes somewhere else! *Satan is always wary of interfering with me when my heart is full of the happiness and joy of the Holy Spirit.*

ARE YOU EXPERIENCING SORROW?
PRAYER CAN MAKE YOUR TIME OF AFFLICTION
ONE OF STRENGTH AND SWEETNESS.
ARE YOU EXPERIENCING HAPPINESS?
PRAYER CAN ADD A HEAVENLY
FRAGRANCE TO YOUR TIME OF JOY.

—Farrar

Holiness appears to me to have a sweet, calm, pleasant, charming, and serene nature, all of which brings an inexpressible purity, radiance, peacefulness, and overwhelming joy to the soul. In other words, holiness makes the soul like a field or garden of God, with every kind of pleasant fruit and flower, and each one delightful and undisturbed, enjoying a sweet calm and the gentle and refreshing rays of the sun.

—Jonathan Edwards

We always enjoy looking down a long road lined with beautiful trees. *The trees are a delightful sight and seem to be forming a temple of plants, with strong wooden pillars and arches of leaves.* In the same way you look down a beautiful road like this, why not look back on the road of the years of your life? *Look at the large green limbs of God's mercy overhead and the strong pillars of his loving-kindness and faithfulness that have brought you much joy.* Do you see any birds singing in the branches? If you look closely, surely you will see many, for they are singing of God's mercy received "thus far."

—Charles H. Spurgeon

With singing lips my mouth will praise you. —Psalm 63:5

BE LIKE A BIRD THAT, HALTING IN ITS
FLIGHT, RESTS ON A LIMB TOO SLIGHT.
AND FEELING IT GIVE WAY BENEATH HIM SINGS,
KNOWING HE HAS WINGS.

Do you believe that your heavenly Father will let you carry the banner of his victory and joy to the very front of the battle, only to calmly withdraw to see you captured or beaten back by the enemy? Never! His Holy Spirit will sustain you in your bold advance and fill your heart with gladness and praise.

Not a single blow can hit,

Till the God of love sees fit.

Do not be afraid to enter the cloud descending on your life, for God is in it. *And the other side is radiant with his glory.* "Do not be surprised at the painful trial you are suffering, as though something strange were happening to you. *But rejoice that you participate in the sufferings of Christ*" (1 Peter 4:12–13). When you feel the most forsaken and lonely, God is near. *He is in the darkest cloud.* Forge ahead into the darkness without flinching, knowing that under the shelter of the cloud, God is waiting for you.

He who dwells in the shelter

of the Most High

will rest in the shadow

of the Almighty. —Psalm 91:1

Isn't there something captivating about the sight of a person burdened with many trials, yet who is as lighthearted as the sound of a bell? Isn't there something contagious and valiant in seeing others who are greatly tempted but are "more than conquerors" (Romans 8:37)? Isn't it heartening to see a fellow traveler whose body is broken, yet who retains the splendor of unbroken patience? What a witness these give to the power of God's gift of grace!

—Dr. J. H. Jowett

IN THE HOLY HUSH OF THE EARLY DAWN
I HEAR A VOICE—
"I AM WITH YOU ALL THE DAY,
REJOICE! REJOICE!"

Sing to the Lord, always giving thanks
to God the Father for everything.

—Ephesians 5:19-20

It is not difficult for the Lord to turn night into day.

He who sends the clouds can just as easily clear the skies.

Let us be encouraged—things are better down the road.

Let us sing God's praises in anticipation of things to come.

—Charles H. Spurgeon

I had recently received bad news from home, and deep shadows of darkness seemed to cover my soul. I prayed but the darkness remained.

I forced myself to endure but the shadows only deepened. Then suddenly one day, as I entered a missionary's home at an inland station, I saw these words on the wall: "Try giving thanks." So I did, and in a moment every shadow was gone, never to return. Yes, the psalmist was right: "It is good to praise the LORD" (Psalm 92:1).

—Rev. Henry W. Frost

FOR YOU MAKE ME GLAD

BY YOUR DEEDS, O LORD;

I SING FOR JOY

AT THE WORKS OF YOUR HANDS.

—Psalm 92:4

WAIT AT GOD'S PROMISE
UNTIL HE MEETS YOU THERE,
FOR HE ALWAYS RETURNS
BY THE PATH OF HIS PROMISES.

joy

Begin the day with God! He is your Sun and Day!

His is the radiance of your dawn; To him address your day.

Sing a new song at morn! Join the glad woods and hills;

Join the fresh winds and seas and plains,

Join the bright flowers and rills.

Sing your first song to God! Not to your fellow men;

Not to the creatures of his hand, But to the glorious one.

Take your first walk with God! Let him go forth with thee;

By stream, or sea, or mountain path,

Seek still his company.

Your first transaction be, With God himself above;

So will your business prosper well, All the day be love.

—Horatius Bonar

JESUS CHRIST IS NOT MY SECURITY
AGAINST THE STORMS OF LIFE,
BUT HE IS MY PERFECT SECURITY IN THE STORMS.
HE HAS NEVER PROMISED ME AN EASY PASSAGE,
ONLY A SAFE LANDING.